Product Creation

15 Essential Products for More Profits in Your Business

Julia A. Royston

BA, MA, MLS, DRE

BK Royston Publishing
P. O. Box 4321
Jeffersonville, IN 47131
502-802-5385
http://www.bkroystonpublishing.com
bkroystonpublishing@gmail.com

© Copyright – 2020

All Rights Reserved. No part of this book may be reproduced, stored in a retrieval system, or transmitted by any means without the written permission of the author.

Cover Design: Gad Savage, Elite Covers

ISBN-13: 978-1-951941-11-6

Printed in the United States of America

Dedication

I dedicate this book to anyone who has wanted to or currently owns a business. Whatever business that you are in, some or all of these products will help you grow and expand your business.

Let's go!

Acknowledgements

First, I acknowledge my Lord and Savior Jesus Christ for giving me all of my gifts and especially my gift to write His words.

My husband who is always supportive, loving and encouraging me to utilize all of my gifts and talents. Thank you honey.

To my mother, Dr. Daisy Foree, who is my number one cheerleader and always tells me, "hang in there, you can do it." To my father, Dr. Jack Foree, who is never far away from me in spirit or my heart. I only have to look in the mirror each day to see him.

To Rev. Claude and Mrs. Lillie Royston, Michael and Jean Royston who support me in everything I do.

To the rest of my family, I love you and thank you for your prayers, support and love.

To My Business Bestie Vanessa Collins and all of the other "Business Queens" in the virtual and global world. I dedicate this to you. We work long and hard each day. I pray that you are profitable and prosperous in whatever business that you are pursuing. Blessings.

Table of Contents

Dedication	iii
Acknowledgements	v
Introduction	ix
Book	1
eBook	5
Audiobook	9
Workbook	13
Planner/Checklist	17
Journal	21
Workshop	25
Course	29
Videos	35
Audios	39
Blog	43
Podcast	47
Online eCommerce Store	51

Social Media Presence	57
Signature Speech	63
About the Author	57

Introduction

I've been in business at the printing of this book for 12 years. I didn't really intend to be in business because my father was a teacher/entrepreneur and my mother helped him in the business along with me and my two sisters. It's what I've grown up doing. I didn't pick or choose it, it chose me.

Over time, I have realized that the more products or even variety of products that I have to sell, the more people I can sell to.

Like the large chain stores and outlets across the country, the more different products they have to sell the greater potential they have for someone to buy something.

On the other hand, there are never any sales guarantees but I promise you that you will sell more, if you have more to sell. My purpose for writing this book is to give you 15 of the essential products that I have to lead people to me and if interested and I meet a need, they will buy something else from me. Some people buy my books right away. Others have to be convinced over time that my content is worth their time and money. That's okay, I've got plenty of content and creating more every day, hence this book.

If you don't have many products to sell or wonder why some people don't buy from you, it may be that they don't know how important your product is to the betterment of their life. Start there and I gave you that one for free.

Let's find out what we need to create.

Book

As you might guess, we start off with books. Every person has a story to tell and your business has a back story, history and perspective on the industry that it represents. Your business needs a book. If you have not written a book, I encourage you to do so. If you need help doing so, reach out to me. Why? A book is your voice to the world. It puts in printed form what you want to say related to your business, expertise and industry. It also leaves a legacy even after you have departed this life. Also, your book can help you build your platform, brand your identity and gives you industry credibility. So, you say that you have one book? Great. But, where is your second book? I know that I am pushing it but I'm a publisher, books are what I do and can you write, publish and promote your book as well.

I do want to point that in addition to book sales, your book can also be a lead magnet which is an entry into an even large sales funnel and long-term client interaction for more sales and engagement.

If you would like to know more information about creating, publishing and promoting a book or more than one book, let's talk at visit http://www.talkwithroyston.com.

If you need more resources about writing, publishing or promoting your book, visit http://www.bkroystonstore.com

Or visit www.juliaroystonstore.com to purchase any of my books.

Product Use: Lead Magnet, Product Inventory, Up Sell in a Funnel, Textbook for a Workshop, Course or Conference

What type of book do you want to write?

eBook

Some years ago, there were a multiplicity of articles stating that the eBooks would replace the printed book. It is not so and hasn't happened at the release of this book. What has happened is the need for an eBook to accompany your print book. I do believe that you will always need a book but books need to be in multiple formats to reach multiple audiences. The ability to have a book on your computer, laptop, tablet and phone as well as a paperback or hardback to read on the beach is vastly growing. Presently, all of my book publishing packages include both a paperback and electronic format. It is now standard and not an option. I believe that the more media formats that your message is available, there should be more opportunities for a larger audience.

eBooks can also be used in your business in multiple ways. You can sell them on your website, along with a class, workshop or conference or simply produce something short enough to be a lead magnet or give a way. If you are new or establishing your credibility in your industry area, people are more likely to give you their email address in exchange for your eBook rather than purchasing the eBook.

For more information on creating eBooks for your business, visit http://www.bkroystonstore.com and sign up for the eBooks for Business Course this available for independent study.

Product Use: Freemium, Lead Magnet, Product Inventory, Up Sell in a Funnel, Textbook for a Workshop, Course or Conference, Bonus Product for a Membership or Mentorship

What topic will you write about in an eBook? The number of pages can be from 5-10. What will you talk about?

_____
_____
_____
_____
_____
_____
_____
_____
_____
_____
_____
_____
_____
_____
_____
_____
_____
_____
_____
_____

Audiobook

The largest demand in the literary world right now is for audiobooks. People now want to the book to talk to them and they just listen. Now for me, listening to a book is a bed time story and I am preparing for the bed. My husband assures me that I won't get sleepy when I am listening to a book. I'm not convinced but to each his own. I do know that high quality, professionally narrated and engineered audio recordings are in great demand. You can always utilize these audio recordings just like a music CD, individual tracks or chapter recordings can be bundled with other industry materials and these materials can be used as a gift in a membership, mentorship or other monthly paid programs.

Don't wait. Record it yourself or pay someone to record it for you, and don't miss out on money or the responses from those who will love your story in audio format.

For more information on how to record and/or produce audiobooks, reach out to us and lets have a conversation with one of the BK Royston Publishing team, http://www.talkwithroyston.com.

For independent or self-study regarding audiobooks, visit http://www.bkroystonstore.com

Product Use: Freemium, Lead Magnet, Product Inventory, Bundled item for a Bonus Product for a Membership or Mentorship

What type of book have your written that can be easily be turned into an audiobook?

_____
_____
_____
_____
_____
_____

Do you have empowerment quotes or social media posts that you do daily that can be easily and quickly transferred to audio?

_____
_____
_____
_____
_____
_____
_____
_____
_____
_____

Workbook

The first word in the word "workbook" perfectly describes for me what a workbook is, a working book or something that you are working through to achieve or complete a particular goal or project. I have written several workbooks including a workbook to teach and walk you through exactly how to write a book. I have written a workbook that accompanied a devotional and main book so that the instructor and/or reader can dive deeper into the subject matter, reflect, create, decide and come out with a great understanding of the subject after having read the text. You can sketch, brainstorm and work out a lot of problems and issues before you start a project in the workbook.

If you are a financial investor or represent real estate company, workbooks are perfect for working through and getting a better understanding of the numbers.

For more information on how to create your own workbook, reach out to us at, http://www.talkwithroyston.com. To purchase any of Julia Royston's workbooks they are located at: http://www.juliaroystonstore.com

Product Use: Freemium, Lead Magnet, Product Inventory, Accompanying book to an existing book, Textbook for a Workshop, Course or Conference, Bonus Product for a Membership or Mentorship

What is a new idea for a book and/or workbook that can be a combined resource? Do you already have an idea for a workbook from a previous study or course?

_____
_____
_____
_____
_____
_____
_____
_____
_____
_____
_____
_____
_____
_____
_____
_____
_____

Planner/Checklist

In certain businesses and industries, there are pieces of information, documentation and reports that are needed throughout the process. If the client had the documents or information handy, don't you think that the process would move much smoother? Of course, it would. Additionally, there are people that know that they need a will, power of attorney or a house and they don't want information is needed on their part to begin or complete the process. The fear of the unknown or the rejection that they don't have the right documents or money needed or whatever is necessary at times, keeps people from getting the help that they need from you the service/business provided.

Ease their mind and bring clients to you faster and easier by providing a checklist or planner with the information that they need to get started or complete the process. Get their contact information so that you can keep in touch with them while they are gathering the information. Your help with the free checklist or planner will make this process easier and quicker. Additionally, with this vital information, it will help you in the long run have a more informed client and hopefully, a satisfied client and profitable sale.

For more information on creating checklists for your business, schedule a time at http://www.talkwithroyston.com.

Product Use: Freemium, Lead Magnet, Promotional and Information material for events, trade shows and informative workshops.

What type of information is needed for a helpful business checklist?

_____
_____
_____
_____
_____
_____
_____
_____
_____
_____
_____
_____
_____
_____
_____
_____
_____
_____
_____
_____

Journal

I wrote my first book from the simple spiral 80-page notebooks from the discount store. I just wrote what was on my mind and in my heart. So, the practice of journaling is very therapeutic and helpful for the mind, body and spirit.

You as a business owner/author can create your own journal that can contain blank pages with a decorative cover. Other types of journals can accompany devotionals or inspirational writings where people can write down their thoughts, reflections and directions for the next steps based on the devotional lesson.

You can also create journals that accompany a process, strategy, project or method of creating something. For example, you can create a weight loss or eating or food journal for a membership program. If you are a realtor, you can have a new home owner journal for the process of owning and moving into their first home.

There are so many ways to create, use and bundle journals with existing products and services. Create your own journal today.

The latest inspirational journal from Julia Royston accompanies her Queen inspirational book. Purchase the Queen book and journal at http://www.juliaroystonstore.com.

Product Use: Freemium, Lead Magnet, Product Inventory, Accompanying book to an existing book, Textbook for a Workshop, Course or Conference, Bonus Product for a Membership or Mentorship

What type of Journal do you need to create for your business?

_____
_____
_____
_____
_____
_____
_____
_____
_____
_____
_____
_____
_____
_____
_____
_____
_____
_____
_____
_____
_____
_____

Workshop

What do you know how to do? Whatever that thing, subject, project or skill is, teach it! A workshop is a great way to display what you know to a larger group instead of one on one. The things to consider is whether your audience is willing to attend a live face to face event or a virtual event online from the comfort of their home. Remember that you should charge for the workshop as well. If it is important to people, they should be willing to pay for the workshop. In my experience, people will also engage and appreciate you and your content more, if you charge for the information. You can add a journal, a pen and peppermint for live event, but charge. If you are having a virtual event, charge for it as well, but offer a glam bag or goodie bag to add more value to your virtual event. If you need help developing a workshop, reach out to us at http://www.talkwithroyston.com

Product Use: Lead Magnet for a higher core offer, Your Business and Industry Product, Up sell in a Funnel, Bonus Product Content for a Membership or Mentorship Group

What 2-4 Hour Workshop would you like to teach to your potential client?

_____
_____
_____
_____
_____
_____
_____
_____
_____
_____
_____
_____
_____
_____
_____
_____
_____
_____
_____
_____
_____
_____

List 5 topics that can be taught in a shorter 30-45-minute workshop

_____
_____
_____
_____
_____
_____
_____
_____
_____
_____
_____
_____
_____
_____
_____
_____
_____
_____
_____

Course

Now that you know what a workshop is, imagine taking several workshops or expanding the workshops into a multi-week course. The best courses have come as a result of teaching on a topic and people wanting to know more and dig deeper into a specific topic. First, if a topic is something that I know that people are interested in and that I have a knowledge of, I usually write a book about it. The books I write are either directly related to my business, purpose or interest, period.

If I've written the book, I usually teach from my own books. Why? Because I know the content because I am the author. Secondly, my book is now a textbook that goes directly with my course. Finally, I receive the profit from the book and the 6, 8, 10 or 12-week course.

It has been said that people will pay you for what you know. I also say that you have to be ready to charge them and have the content formatted so that people can be plugged directly into the course quickly and easily.

What do you want to teach people? If there is a specific product that we want to create, a multi-week course is probably the best way to do it. I have a 10-week course on how to write a book. I have a 5-week course on blogging. So again, what do you want to teach people? Always have an end product or end result in mind when you are teaching the course. Have a lesson plan, activity and homework for each week.

For more information on how to create a course from a book, visit http://www.bkroystonstore.com and there is a course already created on "How to Turn Your Book into a

Course." Of course, there is, why wouldn't there be? Lol.

Product Use: Up sell in a Funnel, Core Offer, Bonus Product Content for a Membership or Mentorship Group

What do you want to teach that could easily be a multi-week course?

_____
_____
_____
_____
_____
_____
_____
_____
_____
_____
_____
_____
_____
_____
_____
_____
_____
_____
_____
_____
_____
_____

What workshops have you taught that could easily be bundled into a multi-week course?

Videos

Videos clearly fulfill the saying, 'a picture is worth a thousand words' to the 10th degree. Today, that same picture now has animation, sound, other images, text and music added to make the picture even more appealing and interactive. A video grabs the viewer's attention. A link added to that same video at the beginning, middle and end can add money to the pockets of the producer of the video. Videos should be authentic and don't have to be polished to be effective. We have seen how horrible videos showing murders of innocent people have sparked protests and riots in the streets across this country. We have seen dancers, singers and other artists display their talents and land multi-million-dollar contracts and become world famous.

We have seen educators, coaches and trainers provide video courses, and become famous, profitable and transform lives around the world from their videos. Memories are made, savored and cherished through video. The video commentary surrounding the message of your book should be the introduction to your website, course or program. There are so many ways that video can be used with your book, business and product line that it is a crucial and critical piece of the business equation. It is no longer an option, but a necessity. Whether you utilize a several hundred-dollar HD cameras or your phone, make it meaningful, content-rich and come straight from the heart and watch how it will reach the masses.

Product Use: Freemium, Lead Magnet, Introduction to You, Your Business and Industry Product Inventory, Up sell in a Funnel, Content for a Workshop, Course or Conference

What type of video(s) do you need to create for your business?

Audios

Now audio files are quickly becoming more popular again especially for busy people. They can listen to and learn new content while riding on the train, bus, in their car or while exercising each day. People can be inspired, educated and entertained by the audio files that they listen to.

You can turn these same audio files into an audiobook which we have talked about before or later on we will talk about the ever-increasing business outlet of podcasts.

How do you create an audio file? I use an app on my phone to create audio files. It is quick, easy and in an extremely quiet space, can be uploaded immediately or sent directly to customers, members of a membership or mentorship group as well as added to a blog post or other paid program.

If you don't know what to say, write it down. Practice it multiple times. Speak slowly and clearly into a high definition device in a quiet space. There you have it an audio file that can motivate, stimulate and inspire millions.

If you have questions or need help, reach out at http://www.bkroystonstore.com.

Product Use: Freemium, Lead Magnet, Product Inventory, Bundle with another product for a give-away, Content for a Workshop, Course or Conference, Bonus Product Content for a Membership or Mentorship Group

What type of audio files would benefit your clients?

BLOG

Blogging to some is not really a product or service. Some of your may feel that blogging has gone out of style but I beg to differ. You still need a way to communicate your thoughts and ideas with your current and potential clients.

I blog on a weekly basis and post them to my websites, email list and portions to my social media sites. I have expanded my blog posts to articles, lead magnets and chapters of books. I repurpose all of my content and never consider any content as a waste of time or effort. Content is always king in a business.

What is blogging? Blogging is a short 250-500 article or content that can be related to your business, life experiences, travel, products, services, reviews and/or anything else you want to talk about. My blog directly attached to my website so that I only have to post once and meet two needs at once. There are people who have separate blog sites from their website but for me, I need to condense my work load and efforts in the best way possible. But with blogging, I can promote a new book release, product or service. I can interview others and they are my guests on my blog. I can always sell products and services via my blog site with direct links to my ecommerce store or sales pages for upcoming events, virtual or in-person.

These same blog posts can be sent directly to your email list or used in a newsletter, magazine or social media posts.

If you need help, I have created a course to help you on your blogging journey at http://www.bkroystonstore.com.

Product Use: Freemium, Lead Magnet, Business, Product and/or Event Promotional Resource, Content that can be bundled for an inspirational book or journal, Bonus and Bundled with an audio and/or video as Product Content for a Membership or Mentorship Group

What topic(s) would you like to blog about?

_____
_____
_____
_____
_____
_____
_____
_____
_____
_____
_____
_____
_____
_____
_____
_____
_____

Podcast

Podcasting has become one of the fastest growing ways to communicate to an audience. We have talked about audio and video but with my podcast, I have combined both. I stream my podcast but also video tape it so that I can use it on my website and/or YouTube channel. I told you earlier that I strive to repurpose content as much as possible. Podcasting also is a way to have a broadcast/telecast that can be repurposed on other Internet based platforms for syndication as well as used again on traditional radio as re-recorded content. Content is king. Adding noteworthy and informative guests can only enhance your podcast. For me, it is a way to train and teach authors, business owners and other organizational leaders how to interact with the media as well as give them an outlet to promote their upcoming releases, events and other products and services.

My podcast/broadcast is "Live Your Best Life" and it is a podcast where I present guests that provide information, entertainment and empowerment for people to actually live their best life. I wanted to the topics open and not just focus on writing or publishing but be able to talk about anything that interests me and my listening audience. Fortunately, I travel, meet people and have clients so willing to be my guest. I am very blessed. I was approached with the idea and gladly accepted because it helps others to be their best self. It also introduces more people to me, my business and my clients.

If you need help, reach out.

Product Use: Freemium, Lead Magnet, Business, Product and/or Event Marketing and Promotional Resource

What would make a great topic for your Podcast?

Online/e-Commerce Store

Who wouldn't want to have their own store that they can sell merchandise anytime day or night? You don't even have to be awake to sell your merchandise. When you wake up someone has bought something, you have a notice of the sale, the shipper will deliver it and you enjoy the profits from the sale. Easy right? Not so fast. Just like any other retail outlet you have to have inventory that people want to buy and you have to have a promotional strategy to get in front of potential customers. The biggest consumer of your time is getting creating the merchandise and organizing your store. There are some made for you ecommerce websites that can help with the organizational part but you have to create the products. After that, the next biggest part is promoting your store. As you can tell, I have been promoting my stores throughout this book. That is only one way to promote your store because as many people as I would like to buy this book, all may not want the information in this book so they won't see my ads for my store. I promote my store on my business cards, blog posts, newsletter, magazine, social media and my websites.

Keeping more of your profits is a primary reason why I have my own ecommerce store. Why? When you have distribution through someone else, no matter how large the distribution outlet, they require and take a portion of your profits as a distribution fee. Right so, because they have bills, expenses for upkeep, shipping, handling and taxes that they have to pay as well as the distributor. On the other hand, if you have your own store and have created digital or physical products, you don't pay the middle man except what you pay to have the store access. Most of the time, there is no fee that you would pay unless someone buys something from you and that is primarily because of the credit card fees. Credit card fees are still less than distribution fees, so you as the owner of the store are able to retain more of your profits when you have a store and sell directly to your customer than if you went through a distributor. You still have to promote to your store and the distributor but if you promote to both, double the exposure and double the profits. If you need help selecting or putting up your store, reach out. Let's go!

Product Use: Freemium, Lead Magnet, Product, Services, Merchandising and/or Event Sales

What products do you have that could be selling in an online store?

Social Media Presence

When people who come to me and ask me about publishing their books, helping them with their business or organization, I usually go to social media first. I want to see what they are telling, showing or displaying for the world to see. Social Media is where I conduct business. I display some personal aspects of my life but my primary goal on social media is for people to get to know me, my business, my products and services.

Now I know you are asking yourself why social media? It's not a product or service that I own. True we don't own social media but we can present, promote and profit from being active on social media with our products, services, business and organizational resources.

With that being said, pick two. I am not talking about the lottery numbers. I am talking about two social media outlets. Two outlets that you will be diligent in learning about, posting and engaging with others to prosper and move forward your book, business and organization. That's it. It is no longer an option but a requirement.

I don't know if you realize it or not but some companies view your social media page before they hire, promote or interview you. Be careful what you post but also, I have had event promoters not allow me to participate in an event because I didn't have high enough social media likes and followers on a certain outlet. It does matter.

My last soap box about social media is if you are participating in an event and they have a flyer or webinar or video, post it, share it and spread the word about it. It helps you and everyone else. Just a hint, people will want to do more business, collaborate and partner with you when you share.

Here are my social media outlets and handles. Follow, Like and Share.

Facebook: @juliaaroyston

Instagram: @juliaaroyston

Twitter: @juliaakroyston

LinkedIn: @juliaaroyston

Product Use: Freemium, Lead Magnet, Webinars, LIVE Events, Product, Services, Merchandising and/or Event Sales, Empowerment Posts,

What are you currently on Social Media?

_____
_____
_____
_____
_____
_____
_____
_____
_____
_____
_____
_____
_____
_____
_____
_____
_____
_____
_____
_____
_____
_____

What do you want to learn more about regards to Social Media?

_____

_____

_____

_____

_____

_____

_____

_____

_____

_____

_____

_____

_____

_____

_____

_____

_____

_____

_____

_____

_____

_____

Signature Speech

An event planner calls you in a panic because the keynote speaker's plane was delayed by weather. The keynote speaker will not be able to make to the conference of 5,000 people and the conference starts in 2 hours. The event planner assures you that you have 20 minutes to speak on a subject that you are a specialist in and to add a little spice to my story, the original key note speaker is one of your mentors. Get the picture? Great. What can you speak on and be effective, deliver, bring your books, sell them in the back of the room (Rules #1 always keep inventory) and have people sign up for your email list? Note to self. Always have an email list. Don't have an email list.

Reach out to me at http://www.talkwithroyston.com. Now with the rest of my story. The event planner goes on to tell you that probably 3-5 people will ask you to speak at a future event because they are look for speakers. What do you speak about? What are you an expert in and don't need to do research or go into a panic mode that can be delivered out of the park in 20 minutes?

That's your signature speech. My signature speech is anything related to writing, publishing, promoting and creating products and services for your business. That's it. I have spoken on this topic a number of times. I have a signature product series that accompanies it. That's how much I do it. That's how many people have asked me about these topics and I consider myself an expert in these topics.

Need help with your signature speech, let's talk.

Product Use: Freemium, Lead Magnet, Webinars

Write out 4 critical points of your signature speech.

About the Author

Julia Royston spend her days doing what she loves, writing, publishing, speaking and coaching others to tell, introduce and create ways to deliver their stories and messages to the world. That is her "Why." BK Royston Publishing LLC, Julia Royston.net, Royal Media and Publishing and Royston Book Fairs are the conduits that she and her husband, Brian Royston use to spread the love of reading, writing, books as well as build businesses around the world. To date, Julia has written 55 books, recorded 3 music CDs and Coached 150+ to write and publish books as well as established their own businesses. Follow her on social media or visit www.bkroystonpublishing.com or www.juliaroyston.net for more information and upcoming events.

www.ingramcontent.com/pod-product-compliance
Lightning Source LLC
Chambersburg PA
CBHW051703090426
42736CB00013B/2517